BRIDGING THE GENERATIONAL DIVIDE: MILLENNIALS AND BOOMERS

HUMANISTIC COMMUNICATION STRATEGIES TO HELP BRIDGE GENERATIONAL DIVIDES

A HUMANIST LEARNING SYSTEMS COMPANION BOOK

By Jennifer Hancock

Edited by Dale McGowan

Published by Jennifer Hancock
Copyright 2018 by Jennifer Hancock
Published 2018

KDP Edition
ISBN: 9781728627434
Imprint: Independently published
Title: Bridging the Generational Divide: Millennials and Boomers
Author: Jennifer Hancock
Editor: Dale McGowan
Publisher: Humanist Learning Systems.

This book is also available in print at most online retailers

All rights reserved. No part of this book may be used or reproduced in any manner whatsoever without written permission, except in the case of brief quotations embodied in critical articles or reviews.

TABLE OF CONTENTS

Chapter 1: Why this Book?.................... 5

    Overview.. 6

    4 learning objectives 6

Chapter 2: What do we know?............. 7

    Definitions.. 7

    What do we know?............................ 8

    Personality Traits 10

    Generalizations 11

Chapter 3: How are we different?....... 15

    Knowledge and Experience 15

    Boomers 17

    Millennials 19

    What Differences Matter?............... 20

Chapter 4: Dignity and Respect 27

    Dignity and Respect 27

    On Being Human 30

The Golden Rule Understood 32

The Impact of Compassion 35

Chapter 5: Communication Strategies 41

Communication Strategies 41

The World Doesn't Revolve Around You 43

Step Back and Listen 47

Don't Win – Solve Problems 49

Don't Fake It 53

Chapter 6: About the Author: 57

More Learning from Jennifer Hancock 58

CHAPTER 1: INTRODUCTION: WHY THIS BOOK?

In this book, we will discuss the research on generational differences and consider how we might use the knowledge to create more effective communication strategies. At the core of this approach is a humanistic respect for the dignity and worth of each human in your company.

This is the companion book to the online course **Bridging the Generational Divide: Millennials and Boomers.** It contains transcripts of the course for easy home reference. Individuals and groups can benefit from this course. For more information, visit:

https://humanistlearning.com/generationaldivide/

Overview

Diversity has many dimensions. Its root is difference -- specifically how we manage differences between people. If you have a big enough business, you have employees that range from young 20-somethings to people of retirement age. These "differences" are generalizations. There is no stereotypical Baby Boomer, and there is no stereotypical Millennial.

4 learning objectives

The four chapters will focus on understanding the following:

1) What we know about the different generations.
2) The stereotypical life experiences of people in different age groups.
3) That despite the differences in age, humans don't vary all that much.
4) Specific strategies to help you communicate more effectively with people different from you.

~~~~~

CHAPTER 2: WHAT DO WE KNOW?

We can't begin to bridge what divides us until we know what exactly that is. This chapter will look into what is actually known about the different generations.

Definitions

Researchers looking at generations must begin by defining the groups they are looking at. Though five generations are generally considered in the research, two of those (the Silent Generation and the Greatest Generation) are primarily out of the workforce. For now, let's focus on who is still in the workforce.

Millennials, who were born after 1980, are in their early 20s through mid-30s and are relatively early in their careers. Generation X -- my generation -- were born between the Baby Boom (which resulted in the Boomers) and the Baby Boomlet (the children the Boomers had when they grew up). The Boomers were born after WWII when people could start having families again.

(Quick note – these terms for the generations are very specific to Western European and American cultures. Other parts of the world are not necessarily broken up into these age cohorts.)

These age groupings are a result of the shared experiences after WWII in the Western allied nations. Whenever an event like a war disrupts normal human relationships, you can see these dips and bulges in the population. These major events also have a profound impact on society in terms of job availability, safety, and more, which leads to the shared experiences of certain age cohorts.

What do we know?

There has actually been quite a bit of research on generational differences, including research from the Pew Research Center and *Psychology Today*.

http://www.pewresearch.org/topics/millennials/

https://www.psychologytoday.com/files/attachments/4330/npitimeupdatespps.pdf

Let's look at some of these results.

College education is one area of difference: 13% of boomers got a college degree compared with 15% of Millennials. A greater difference is apparent when you focus on women: Only 11% of Boomer women got a college degree compared with 20% of Millennial women.

Differences in attitudes about parenting are quite small: 50% of older folks say being a good parent is important to them, and 52% of Millennials do. Same with helping others: 20% of Boomers think this is important compared with 21% of Millennials.

What is interesting in the research is just how similar we are despite the age differences. Humans on the whole need good social relationships, family, and financial security, and that's reflected in the research. We just don't vary that much when it comes to our values. We do have differences, but not in what we value.

Personality Traits

There was a big deal made about a study on narcissistic personality traits in the *Journal of Social Psychological and Personality Science* published in 2010. It showed that Millennials were more narcissistic than the older generations at a similar point in their careers. This research looked at college students when they were in college. When Boomers were in college, 15 to 16% of them scored high on the Narcissistic Personality Inventory (NPI), while 17% of Millennials scored high on the NPI while in college -- a negligible difference.

Here's a better way to think about this: ~85% of Boomers are NOT narcissistic and ~83% of Millennials are NOT narcissistic. What this means for you is that age doesn't really matter. The overwhelming majority of people you meet in your life, regardless of their age, are probably not narcissistic.

Bottom line: Don't ever look at studies that show one group is different or worse personality-wise than another group and believe them. Look at the data and see what it really says. In almost every case, the differences are minuscule. In terms of personality traits, we are far more alike than different. That's because we are all humans who evolved to have pretty much the same genetic profile.

Now let's look at trust. According to a Pew Research study on social trends (http://www.pewsocialtrends.org/files/2010/10/millennials-confident-connected-open-to-change.pdf), 32% of older people think most people are trustworthy, while 28% of Millennials feel the same way. a "whopping" 4% difference. Regardless of age, when you meet someone you have a 70% chance of them thinking you are basically good and trustworthy and a 30% chance of them not being trusting at all. Once again, on this metric, age doesn't really matter.

Generalizations

What I want you to get out of this research is a recognition that most of the "differences" we talk about between the generations are generalizations. There is no stereotypical Baby Boomer and there is no stereotypical Millennial.

Millennials are more narcissistic than Boomers. But only slightly. Not enough to even be considered a difference. Yes, Boomers are more trusting than Millennials, but again, not by much.

Don't ever look at reports of studies that show one group is different or worse personality wise than another group and believe them. Even IF there were a big difference, that still doesn't tell you anything about the individual standing in front of you. Without putting them through a series of personality assessments (most of which have no basis in science), you have no idea where on the scale of personality traits they are anyway.

Here is another way we are more alike than different: Whatever age group you are in, you probably think yours is the best and that all the other ones are flawed. The same studies that show us how "different" we are also show us that 58% of Boomers think their generation is unique and special and 61% of Millennials think the same thing.

In other words, while we are actually quite alike, we like to think we are different, and it's this belief in nonexistent differences that is causing most of our problems.

As it happens, the only group that is humble about their generation is mine! Only 49% of Generation X thinks our generation is special. That's a 10-point difference, which is actually pretty significant.

We are for the most part right. In terms of personality traits, we are much more alike than we are different.

~~~~~

CHAPTER 3: HOW ARE WE DIFFERENT?

While we learned in the previous chapter that there aren't any huge differences in personality traits in the different age groups, that doesn't mean the groups aren't different. In this chapter we will discuss the knowledge and likely life experiences of people in different age ranges. A person's experiences can have a huge impact on how they act and how they respond to and perceive the world.

Knowledge and Experience

So what do we know?

The state of the economy and our economic prospects has a huge impact on how secure we feel. If you come of age in a time of abundance, you come to expect it. Opportunities are everywhere. If you come of age in a depression, you never stop worrying about having enough.

Likewise, your career trajectory is impacted by the economic situation that exists when you enter the workforce. If you are only able to get low-skilled low-wage jobs early in your career, that will follow you for the rest of your life and impact your earnings for the rest of your life.

This in turn colors your view of what society is and what you can or cannot expect from society. Think of this as a measure of societal trust.

The other thing that is different is our cultural experiences. What music was popular? What TV shows? Did you have a phone? What sort of work did people get? What did you eat and how did you prepare your food growing up?

Society has experienced a tremendous amount of social change over the decades, and where we see differences has to do with the cultural experience people have when growing up and coming of age. Personality-wise, we are pretty much all the same. Culturally, we are all over the map.

Boomers

Let's start with The Boomers.

Boomers were literally part of a baby boom. They bulged the population, and that bulge has transformed society as they have moved through it into different life stages.

Boomers probably grew up in a suburban community and had a tremendous amount of freedom as children, freedom Millennials never experienced. Boomers were allowed to play with knives and build things and hang out without adult supervision. They were one of the first generations to have spending money as kids, which in turn fueled a consumer boom. Their parents had jobs. The economy was growing. There was excess money that could be spent on leisure.

On the other hand, there were a lot of them. Their schools were crowded, and they had to compete for everything. But because the economy was growing well into the 70s, people could get good, stable jobs that paid well which allowed them to amass wealth and consume consumer goods like cars and TVs and take vacations.

If there was a telephone in the house, it was one phone that everyone had to share, and it was a landline. You didn't have a choice of phones. You got what the phone company gave you, probably a rotary dialer.

They also grew up in a time when institutionalized racism and gender segregation were the norm. They were the generation who protested and overturned the culture they grew up in to make things better, but these sorts of cultural habits of segregation and discrimination leave a mark and habits of thinking that are very hard to overcome.

Boomers grew up on rock and roll, like Elvis and the Beatles -- what we now consider "oldies" but was considered "classic rock" when I was growing up.

They watched TV, including shows like Sesame Street.

The defining geopolitical problems were the killing of John F. Kennedy, the Cold War and the Cuban Missile Crisis, which had people literally thinking they could die as a result of a nuclear weapon at any moment! It was scary.

Millennials

The so-called Millennial cohort, the largest generation in American history, was born during a recession, came of age during the booming 1990s, entered the labor market during another recession and then got hit with the collapse of the housing market and economy in 2008. The aftereffects of the economic collapse and the income disparities in society are defining economic issues for this generation. Their economic experience is filled with ups and downs in a way that the Boomers' experience was not.

They have known prosperity, and they also understand that getting a job is largely a crap shoot. It simply doesn't matter how qualified you are: If there aren't enough jobs to go around, employment is hard to find.

Additionally, most of them left college saddled with an insane amount of debt. Because debt and the economy impacts everything – I'm including a link to a study for you on Millennials by the Obama White House:

https://obamawhitehouse.archives.gov/sites/default/files/docs/millennials_report.pdf

Culturally, Millennials grew up with cellphones, the Internet, and instant communication. They are digital natives. Their biggest geopolitical event was Sept 11th. Their entire adult life has been spent in a world that is globally connected and the potential to be killed in a terrorist attack or in a mass shooting (if you live in America) is a very real threat.

What Differences Matter?

If a lot of the differences are insignificant, what are the big differences between Boomers and Millennials? What differences really do matter?

Most of what I am about to share comes from a Pew Social Trend report from 2014.

http://www.pewsocialtrends.org/2014/03/07/millennials-in-adulthood/?utm_expid=53098246-2.Lly4CFSVQG2lphsg-Koplg.0

The biggest difference is a huge drop in social trust -- the trust or confidence that society will take care of you, nurture you, and protect you. According to the study, only 19% of Millennials think other people can be trusted. This compares with 40% of Boomers. The report attributes these low scores to social insecurity and income status. The poorer and more disenfranchised you are from society, the lower your level of social trust.

There are several reasons why Millennials are less trusting of society then Boomers. Boomers grew up in a time of social investment. Millennials did not. Their experience is one of social disinvestment at all levels. Additionally, Millennials have been hit particularly hard by the economy. Finally, they are a more diverse generation than the

Boomers are, and minority groups that have not historically been nurtured or protected by society have less social trust because of their personal experiences with society not investing in them.

Another way they differ is that Millennials are much more politically independent. Whereas 32% of Boomers say they are independents, 50% of Millennials do. Seventy percent of Millennials don't think there is much of a difference between the political parties, while 60% of Boomers think there is a great deal of difference between the parties. Again, a lot of this has to do with the time and place people grew up and what was happening at the time.

While Millennials claim political independence, they vote Democratic by a large margin. This is probably due to their increased levels of social liberalism fueled by the fact that, as a group, they aren't very religious. This brings us to religious differences between the generations, which are very real and have an impact on workplace politics and interpersonal trust.

Let's consider some numbers. Twenty-nine percent of Millennials are religiously unaffiliated, compared to 16% of Boomers. Eleven percent are outright atheists, with another 28% agnostic when it comes to the question of whether or not there is a God, which makes 39% of Millennials who are either agnostic or atheist.

By contrast, only 6% of Boomers are atheist -- half the level of atheism compared to Millennials. Seventy-three percent of Boomers are absolutely certain there is a God, and 55% of them consider themselves to be religious people. Millennials? Only 36% consider themselves to be religious.

This shift in the religious views of the population is huge and it impacts social views, politics and more. It also means in the workplace that there is quite a bit more religious diversity than there used to be. People of faith and for whom faith is important talk differently than people who lack faith or for whom faith isn't important. These differences in how we communicate can cause problems.

It isn't that we value different things. It's more that how we talk about what we value is what is different. Our cultural references that exemplify our core values are different.

Our cultural experiences with gender and racial diversity and economic opportunities differ and so what scares us or makes us insecure differs. Our fears and insecurities as individuals can negatively impact our attempts to communicate with others. Our willingness to listen and be open to differing opinions is entirely dependent on how threatened we may feel in the moment. In fact, most of our communication problems have to do with our fears and how we personally feel we aren't being heard.

The solution to these problems is to respect not necessarily the differences, but the fears that are driven by these differences and to treat everyone you meet with dignity.

In the next chapter we are going to discuss why, given how each person you meet has had unique life experiences, you should treat them with respect, even if you don't like them very much.

~~~~~

CHAPTER 4: DIGNITY AND RESPECT

To recap what we have learned so far. In terms of personality, we are all human. We all have the same basic emotional toolkit, needs, and desires, and the same baseline levels of sanity vs. insanity. What makes us different is our individual life experiences and our cultural experiences, which can vary greatly depending on WHEN you were born and what was happening while you were growing up.

This is why in this chapter we are going to discuss the concept of respect and dignity and how each and every human you meet, even if you dislike them, is worthy of being treated with dignity and respect.

Dignity and Respect

Let's start with the concept of dignity and respect.

Each and every human you meet is an individual. They have their own hopes, dreams and desires, as well as hardships, struggles, fears and loves. This is an amazingly difficult concept for us to grasp. We get it in the abstract, but in reality, most of the 7 billion people on the planet are strangers to us. Heck, most of the people we encounter on our daily commute are strangers to us.

We don't have the mental capacity to know more than 150 people, and of those, we can only really know about 30 people well. This impacts how we relate to and experience other people. Specifically, it makes it hard for us to feel compassion for strangers.

The closer someone is to us, the more they matter to us. The less we know someone, the less they matter to us and the less care we will take in accommodating them and their needs. They are one of the faceless masses to us.

Here is what I want you to understand. Most of the 7 billion people on the planet don't know you. You are one of the faceless masses too. And yet, you matter. We all matter. You matter, I matter, and people you don't know matter -- to someone. This is what dignity and respect are about. It's about recognizing the humanity of each and every individual you come across.

Recognizing that the people you interact with are really real will help you communicate with them more effectively. When you start from a place of respect, of feeling like the people you interact with really matter, then the differences you have with them, whatever they are, are more easily dealt with. The idea is to enter into interactions with other people intentionally recognizing them as humans who have dignity.

That's the ideal, not the reality. This is not something any of us do automatically. We have to remind ourselves to do it. But if you can remind yourself to do it, you will find whatever communication problems you were having go away. Because now you are treating the person with dignity even if you disagree with them.

It really does change everything.

On Being Human

The next thing I want you to understand is that everyone you meet is human. They aren't a robot. They aren't perfect. They are a real human with real insecurities, abilities, disabilities and more.

One of the main reasons we come into conflict with other people is because they don't meet up to our expectations of them. We expect them to be perfect. For us. We expect them to interact with us in a certain way so that OUR lives are made easier. The problem is that humans aren't ever perfect. You certainly aren't perfect, and neither are the people you interact with. We are all flawed.

How does this manifest? Well, think about what makes you mad about other people. If you commute, you get mad because people cut you off, or are in your way, or are taking too long to turn left, or didn't put on their turn signal. All of these things frustrate you because they inconvenience you. The other person isn't behaving optimally and you are suffering as a result. I know you know what I'm talking about.

What would happen if you stopped expecting people to be perfect and accepted them for the flawed human beings they are? Once you let go of your unrealistic expectations that everyone should be perfect for you, life gets A LOT easier.

One of the thing that frustrates us the most about people not behaving ideally is that other people aren't very accommodating or understanding of our own personal needs and flaws. It's like they don't give us any grace room at all to make mistakes. One mistake and that's it! Can't have a bad day – or you will get skewered.

It comes down to this: If you want people to accommodate and understand you, you need to make an effort to understand and accommodate other people and stop holding them to impossible standards and then getting mad at them when they fall short.

The Golden Rule Understood

Which brings us to the Golden Rule: You can't change other people. Wait – the Golden Rule is, – "Do unto others as you would have them do unto you." But it's related to the fact you can't change other people.

We all know the Golden Rule, but very few of us actually manage to live by it. I've come to think the reason we don't live up to this ideal is because our understanding of it is wrong.

The way the rule is phrased seems to be about the other person's needs, not our own. There is no explanation of WHY we should be nice to other people. But if we rephrase this, we can bring out an element of enlightened self-interest in it. In doing so, we realize something really rather important -- that our lives are made easier when we are surrounded by people who are good to us, people who are responsible, ethical, honest and nice. And our lives are made more difficult when the people around us lie, don't get things done that they are supposed to, and can't be trusted.

In order to get the nice people to be nice to us, we need to be nice to them. If we are rude, distrustful, dishonest, and irresponsible, then the nice people of the world won't trust us and our lives will be made more difficult.

So do unto others as you would have them do unto you, not for abstract moral reasons, but so that you can make sure the nice people in the world actually want to do business with you and interact with you!

Now remember what I said about the fact that you can't change other people's behavior? That truth intersects with this one.

It doesn't matter how nice you are or how responsible you are. It doesn't matter how respectful you are of people who are different from you taking the time to not get mad when things don't go the way you wanted. Some people just aren't all that nice, and no amount of you being nice is going to change that. You should still be polite and dignified. Don't let them walk all over you, but don't respond to them by being rude back.

My father always said – if you want to slide through life, try being nice. You cannot make other people behave the way you want them to, but you can choose how you will respond to them. I have always found that really rude people are easily manipulated by politeness. They want to fight, and if you refuse, they lose their footing and you gain the upper hand.

We will talk more about this concept in the next chapter. But this really works. You accept the person for who they are and allow them to be whoever it is they are, even if they are a rude jerk. Don't get worked up. Let it go.

The benefits of this approach are that (a) you won't get all that upset when people turn out to be jerks, and (b) the nice people of the world will notice, despite being in a very difficult situation, that you kept your cool and were nice despite it all.

Want to draw good people to you and to be admired? Behave professionally, ethically, and compassionately when someone else is in your face being a jerk! This tactic is going to come into play in the next chapter when we talk about specific communication strategies.

The Impact of Compassion

So far we have discussed the fact that everyone matters, at least to themselves, including you. We've talked about how everyone is a flawed human, including you. And we've talked about how everyone you meet – including you – would like it if the people they interacted with were nice, ethical and responsible, as that would make their lives better. When we have communication breakdowns, it's usually because we don't feel respected, understood or we feel like we aren't being treated well.

Remember how I said in the second chapter that we humans are more alike than different and that one of the ways we are alike is that we think our particular age cohort is better than the other ones? We're like that because we humans are tribal by nature. Our tribe is good, whatever that tribe is and however that is defined by us, even if our tribe is completely arbitrary. Everyone not in our tribe is "other" and therefore bad. We feel secure when we are in a tribe.

When we are attacked or feel insecure, we tend to retreat to our tribe.

Another trait we have as humans is that we like to rationalize our decisions. It turns out our unconscious brains make all sorts of decisions for us, and we aren't even aware it's happening, because…it's unconscious.

One of the things we aren't aware of is that our brain has biases in favor of some tribal markers and against others. These biases and tribal markers can be gender, age, skin color, clothing style, ethnicity markers, and more. Every time we meet people, our brains size them up for us and places them within our "tribe" which is good, or outside of it, which is bad. And again, you aren't aware your brain is doing this – it's an unconscious rather than conscious bias.

We end up having gut-level instincts about people based not on how this person behaves or who they really are, but on how we think they might behave, guided by our unconscious biases tied to our tribal instincts.

These gut level instincts impact how we treat people. If we deem someone outside our tribe, we are likely to be ruder to them. And they respond to that rudeness with rudeness because that's how humans are. And then we mutually decide we don't like each other, and all communication from that time forward is…kind of poisoned.

I know you've had this experience and felt both disappointed and justified at the same time. This happens when we cross generational divides, gender divides, racial divides, or really any divide. What is actually happening is that our hidden unconscious biased mind is causing us to behave in a disrespectful way. and that has a cascading effect on our communication.

The antidote to this is compassion. When you start to feel frustrated and that you aren't being understood, and that the other person isn't respecting you or that you aren't being treated well, try to take a step back from your emotional reaction and remind yourself: this other person is a human just like I am, and if I am feeling this way, they probably are too.

Feel compassion for yourself being the flawed human you are and that your brain caused you to be so defensive. Feel compassion for the other person because – while they might very well be being rude to you, the likelihood is that you are being rude right back at them.

And then, once you have gotten yourself out of your head enough and activated compassion, resolve to start treating them with dignity. Understand and accept their flaws and strive to treat them well despite your frustration. This is what being a professional is all about.

Transitioning out of a place of frustration into compassion takes a LOT of practice. But if you can muster it, you will feel better about yourself and about the interactions you are having because it really will change everything.

There is a reason why every religion and philosopher throughout history has taught compassion. It's really a powerful emotion and a powerful tool to improve interpersonal interactions. You will find that even if the other person really is a jerk, your compassionate response will help you in those interactions as well.

Compassion is not something you do for the other person. It's something you do for you. The more you practice it, the more you will reap the benefits -- even and especially when dealing with the jerks of the world.

In the next chapter we are going to discuss specific communication strategies you can use when you feel that you aren't being listened to or heard.

~~~~~

CHAPTER 5: COMMUNICATION STRATEGIES

The reason we spent the last chapter talking about the need to treat people with dignity, respect, and compassion is because having the right attitudinal approach is the foundation upon which all good communication is built.

In this chapter, we are going to discuss specific strategies you can use to help ensure you are listening and hearing what other people have to say so that you can be heard and respected as well.

Communication Strategies

Let's talk about specific communication strategies you can employ when you find that you have a communication problem, regardless of what is causing it.

First, it's beneficial to understand where the other person is coming from. We tend to make a lot of assumptions about what other people are thinking and our assumptions are often REALLY bad. This is why the last chapter was so focused on helping you to understand the other person as a human being worthy of dignity and respect despite your frustration with them.

The next communication skill is listening -- really listening to what the other person is telling you. Often we think we know, but we are just assuming we know, so we respond to our assumptions instead of what is actually being said.

If you've ever had someone put words into your mouth, you've experienced this from the other side. If you've ever been accused of putting words into someone's mouth, you are guilty of this yourself.

The next skill is how to ask questions. It turns out that if you want to win a debate, don't debate. Don't try to win. Ask questions instead. We are going to discuss how better to do that to overcome communication problems.

Finally, we are going to talk about the necessity of being real.

The World Doesn't Revolve Around You

Let's start with the fact that the world doesn't revolve around you.

One of the main problems we have when we try to communicate with others is that we have blinders on. We are only really able to experience our life. We can sympathize with others if we make an effort, but we are locked inside our heads.

We experience other people not as they really are but as we perceive them to be. This is problematic in interpersonal relationships because we end up making a lot of assumptions.

We are unable to read other people's minds, so we assume they think like we do. And that means we assume they are responding to the same things we are. Most of the time they aren't. They are responding to the things they are experiencing as individuals. And that might not have anything to do with us, even though we are interacting with them.

Let me give you an example. You are in a checkout line at a store, and the person in front of you is having trouble paying. Do you know why? No. You can make guesses, but you really have no idea.

Are they doing it to intentionally make you late? Probably not, but it's amazing how many people react to these situations as if it's all about them. The other person who is struggling isn't important except as they impact you and make you wait. Obviously that's a very selfish way to react to other people. Yet we all have felt that way at some point. We have to remind ourselves, in the moment, that it's not about us.

They could be starting to suffer from Alzheimer's. They could be broke. They could have just lost a child or a parent. They could be drunk. Or, they could just be a jerk who likes to make people wait. You don't know. All you can do is look at them and come up with a hypothesis. What I want you to understand is that your hypothesis about their behavior is based on your experiences, not theirs. And you are most likely wrong because most of the time we assume that other people are responding to us when they are not.

We do this a lot when we are having a disagreement about something. We are directly interacting with this person. Of course they must be responding to us, right? Except that if you took the time to step back a little bit, you might find that isn't the case. They have their own pressures and situations they are dealing with. Your conversation is intersecting with all that other stuff. If they get short with you – it may not be because of anything you have done. It may be because someone else is putting pressure on them too.

When I am having a communication problem with someone and it appears that they are responding to me negatively, I always find it's a really good idea to take a pause. Remind myself that their behavior, while directed at me, might not have anything to do with me. When I do this, I can start considering what else might be going on with this person.

Most of the time, there is something else going on and when I ask what is going on with them, I transform what was shaping up to be a conflict into an assist. Now I'm in a position to help them solve their problem and my problem at the same time. But I can only do that if I step out of my own head long enough to remember the world doesn't revolve around me, and what is going on with this person probably has nothing to do with me. They have their own stuff going on and they are responding to it as best they can.

Give them the benefit of the doubt before jumping to conclusions.

To put yourself in the right frame of mind, you need to be humble enough to realize you aren't the center of this other person's universe, and you need to be compassionate enough to care about them so that you can find out what the real problem is. If you can muster the humility and compassion to focus on the other person, your communication problems will largely disappear.

Step Back and Listen

Once you have gotten out of your own head, step back and listen.

If you are hiking and you come across an obstacle and you can't get past it. What do you do? Stepping back and seeing if there might be a different way forward would be a good strategy. It's the same with communication. If you reach an impasse with someone, step back and reassess what's going on so you can see if there is another path forward. When you step back, you stop focusing on your goals and start focusing on the obstacle in your path. In this case, it's another human being who is blocking your way. To get past them, you need to understand *why* they are blocking your path.

In order to get this person to work with you, listen to them to find out what it is *they* are responding to, and that means your listening has to be focused on what their needs are.

Most of us really struggle with this. We listen to other people for cues that can help us and our needs. But to do this well, you need to actually not be focused on your needs. You need to be focused on the other person's needs. Otherwise you won't actually hear them. You will instead be filtering what they are saying through your own lens, and you will miss what actually matters to *them*.

So step back from your insecurities and take the time to actually listen to what this other person is saying!

I find it's helpful to me when I reframe this task into a fact-finding mission. I have several questions I need them to answer for me. Asking questions is the best way to get them to talk about themselves and their problems and not focus on me.

Again, this is about me stepping back from the conflict to actually listen. This is about them, not me.

My first questions are, *What is it this person needs? What sort of things are they actually responding to? What is motivating them? What are they afraid of or concerned about? What sort of pressures are they facing to get their job done?* And most importantly, *How can I help them with these problems and can I do so in a way that benefits both of us?*

Never assume you know the answers to these questions. Your assumptions are most likely wrong. Ask and find out what is really driving this person. If you don't, your efforts to fix the communication problem will fail because instead of fixing the real problem, you will be working on fixing what you assume to be the problem.

I don't know about you, but I don't have that sort of time to waste, and I find it incredibly annoying when someone does this to me. It's really condescending, time-consuming, and pointless.

I find it's better and more effective if I just ask: *What's wrong? How can I best help?*

Don't Win – Solve Problems

In order to focus on how to help the other person so that they can help you, you have to not be focused on "winning" the conflict. As long as you are stuck in a me vs. them paradigm, you will not be able to fix your communication problems and you are not going to fix whatever the problem was that you had been attempting to communicate about!

Remember what I said earlier: You need to be humble. Here's where it really matters. In order to be heard and for your ideas to be fully considered and for others to be engaged with you and your work productively, you have to be focused on solving whatever the problem is you are trying to solve. As long as your ego is in the way and you are focused on winning and being right, you won't be working on solving the problem.

I don't know about you, but if my choice is to win an argument or solve my problem, I want to solve my problem. Because, if I solve my problem, I've won. If I fail to solve my problem because I was too busy winning an argument, I've lost.

Don't let your pride get in the way of your ultimate goal – solving your problem.

We are humans. We are competitive. We like to win. And the person you are having communication problems is not any different! They want to win too. And they may very well be combative. If you try to fight them, they will probably fight you.

If, on the other hand, you figure out what they really need and what their real problems are, you can then help them solve their problems and solve yours at the same time. And they will most likely let you because you have made this about them and their needs. You've set yourself up not as an adversary but as a supporter. This has a dramatic impact on how the other person responds to you.

Here's how this technique works. Instead of advocating for whatever it is you are advocating for, STOP. Consider the other person compassionately and ask questions to find out what they are struggling with, and more importantly, why. What problem do they think needs to be solved? And why? Then ask them questions about how their proposed solution will help them solve their problem. Have them consider the pros and cons of their proposal by asking questions.

For instance: If they have a proposed solution, but you believe their solution won't work because of a problem they seem oblivious to, you can tentatively agree with their proposal and then ask them if the problem you are concerned about happens, how do they plan on dealing with it?

Studies have shown that taking this kind of Socratic approach encourages collaborative problem solving. Once you are engaged in collaborative problem solving, getting other people to consider your alternatives and concerns becomes *much* easier. Why? Because instead of approaching the conversation from a me vs. them framework which creates conflict, you have framed the conversation in an us-working-together framework.

Me vs. them is tribal. All your instinctual negative biases come into play when you treat someone as a tribal enemy. When you instead frame things as us working together, you are harnessing your tribal instincts so that positive biases come into play and that makes communication easier.

More importantly, you are triggering these same positive tribal biases in the person you are communicating with and that makes them more willing to communicate with you in a positive way.

Don't Fake It

There is one last thing I want to caution you about: Don't fake it. Don't try to use these techniques to manipulate other people, because that won't work.

Think of a time you had to deal with someone unpleasant. You think to yourself, this person is an idiot." But verbally, you say something polite and the other person responds as if you just insulted them!

Know why that happens? Because most humans are really adept at reading body language and tone of voice. We understand the meaning and the emotional intent even if the content differs.

If you want to improve your communication skills, you have to stop thinking horrible things about other people while trying to communicate with them. Seriously, you won't make much progress until you do. This is why I spent so much time in this book talking about compassion. Even if you don't respect someone, you can still feel compassion for them so that you treat them with dignity. Compassion will help you respond to the person more authentically so that what you want them to hear is what they actually hear.

Consider two different scenarios. The first is when you have to talk to someone who you have butted heads with in the past. I find that if I have had communication problems in the past and that I do have some well-founded biases, acknowledging those biases can be helpful, but only if I'm willing to work past them so that I can work with this person productively.

If I flat out don't trust the person, once again, compassion helps me. I don't think of untrustworthy or pathologically mean people as ogres. I don't go to war with them. I simply work around them. And I feel sorry for them so that my communication with them isn't laced with malice, but with compassion instead.

Again, this isn't something you can fake. If you just can't respect someone, pity them instead and try to think of them compassionately. What you may just find is that when you stop treating them as if they are a threat to you, they will stop responding to you as if you are a threat!

Communication is a two-way street. If you hate someone, they will respond to that hate even if you don't say it out loud. The best way to ensure your communication is as polite and respectful as you would like it to be is to feel compassion – even for the people you hate.

The next situation I want you to consider is how you treat coworkers you don't have a negative history with or with whom you just have a history of communication problems, but no real animosity.

Compassion will help you because *if* you have any instinctual negative biases against this person, that will come out in communication with them. Compassion will help you override those instincts with respect to this particular individual.

Instead of your communication with someone you don't know being laden with whatever negative associations your unconscious brain has put on them unfairly, you will instead communicate with them as if they are a blank slate for you to get to know. Most people respond positively when you take this approach.

Almost everyone has had an experience where someone you don't even know dislikes you immediately. Don't do that to other people, and don't allow your unconscious biases to cause you to do this. If you find yourself disliking someone, question why and give them the benefit of the doubt by invoking your compassion.

I'm including a few links to additional resources in the form of books and other programs you might find helpful.

The Power of Pause – book - https://humanistlearning.com/book-the-power-of-pause/

Socratic Jujitsu – program - https://humanistlearning.com/socratic-jujitsu/

CHAPTER 6: ABOUT THE AUTHOR:

Jennifer Hancock is a mom, author of several books, and founder of Humanist Learning Systems. Jennifer is unique in that she was raised as a freethinker and is considered one of the top speakers and writers in the world of Humanism today. Her professional background is varied including stints in both the for-profit and nonprofit sectors. She has served as Director of Volunteer Services for the Los Angeles SPCA, sold international franchise licenses for a biotech firm, was the Manager of Acquisition Group Information for a half-billion-dollar company, and served as the executive director for the Humanists of Florida. When she became a mother, she decided to stay at home, but that didn't last long. Shortly after her son was born, she published her first book, *The Humanist Approach to Happiness: Practical Wisdom.* Her speaking and teaching business coalesced into the founding of

Humanist Learning Systems which provides online personal and professional development training in humanistic business management and science-based harassment training that actually works.

More Learning from Jennifer Hancock

OTHER BOOKS BY JENNIFER HANCOCK

- The Humanist Approach to Happiness
- Jen Hancock's Handy Humanism Handbook
- The Bully Vaccine
- The Humanist Approach to Grief and Grieving
- How to Win Arguments Without Arguing
- Ending Harassment & Retaliation in the Workplace
- Why Bullies Bully & How to Stop Them Using Science
- Reality Based Decision Making for Effective Strategy Development
- Why Conflict Management Doesn't Work When the Problem is Bullying

- How to De-Escalate Conflicts Using Behavioral Science

COURSES TAUGHT BY JENNIFER HANCOCK
- Workplace Bullying for HR professionals
- Living Made Simpler
- An Introduction to Humanism
- Socratic Jujitsu: How to Win Arguments Without Argument
- Why Conflict Resolution Doesn't Work When the Problem is Bullying
- Bridging the Generational Divide: Millennials vs. Boomers
- Ending Harassment and Retaliation in the Workplace
- Reality Based Decision Making for Effective Strategy Development
- How to De-escalate Conflicts Using Behavioral Science
- Why is Change so Hard?
- Principles of Humanistic Management
- 7 Sins of Staff Management
- How to Handle Cranky Customer Problems
- New Manager Orientation

- [Humanist Group Leadership Lessons](#)
- [Sexual harassment training that works – general](#)
- [Sexual harassment training that works – AB 1825](#)
- [Stop Bullying in our Workplace – Staff Training](#)
- [Sexual Harassment Compliance Training](#)
- [No Fear Act training](#)
- [Planning for Personal Success!](#)
- [Talking to your child about death](#)
- [The Bully Vaccine Toolkit](#)
- [How to talk to your child's school about bullying](#)
- [Why Bullies Bully & How to Stop Them](#)
- [EEO Refresher Course Training](#)

CONNECT WITH ME ONLINE:
- Twitter: http://twitter.com/#!/JentheHumanist
- Facebook: http://www.facebook.com/JentheHumanist
- Or sign up for my mailing list: http://eepurl.com/c3LuI

Sign up for a course at
https://humanistlearning.com

The End

#####

www.ingramcontent.com/pod-product-compliance
Lightning Source LLC
Chambersburg PA
CBHW071433220526
45469CB00004B/1510